Let's Find Out

Let's Find Rain Forest Animals:
Up, Down, Around

Janice Behrens

Scholastic Inc.
New York Toronto London Auckland
Sydney Mexico City New Delhi
Hong Kong Buenos Aires

Literacy Specialist: Francie Alexander, Chief Academic Officer, Scholastic Inc.
Art Director: Joan Michael

Photographs: ©Royalty-Free/Corbis (red-eyed treefrog); ©Renee Lynn/Corbis (tiger); ©W. Perry Conway/Corbis (orangutan); ©Michael & Patricia Fogden/Corbis (anteater); ©Michael Durham/DRK Photos (frog); ©Timothy Laman/National Geographic/Getty (snake); ©Michael & Patricia Fogden/Minden Pictures (toucan); ©Martin Harvey/DRK Photo (lizard); ©Tom Brakerfield/Digital Vision/Getty (jaguar); ©Reinhard Dirscheri/Alamy (butterfly); ©Mickey Gibson/Animals Animals (macaws)
All word photos: James Levin

ISBN 0-439-91579-1

2 3 4 5 6 7 8 9 10   62   14 13 12 11 10 09 08 07

What is behind the leaves?

The tiger is **behind** the leaves.

behind

What is between the trunks?

The orangutan is **between** the trunks.

between between

What is
on
the branch?

The anteater is on the branch.

What is under the leaf?

The frog is **under** the leaf.

under

What is around the branch?

The snake is around the branch.

around

What is inside the tree?

The toucan is **inside** the tree.

inside

What is going up the tree?

The lizard is going up the tree.

What is going **down** the log?

The jaguar is going **down** the log.

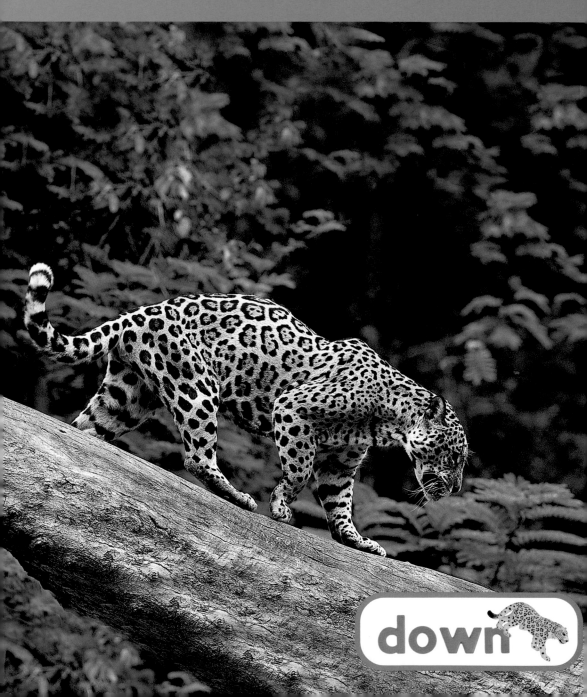

down

What is
above
the flowers?

The butterfly is **above** the flowers.

above

What is beside the macaw?

Other macaws are beside the macaw.

beside

Read-Aloud Animal Facts

Share some fun facts about each creature in this book.

Bengal Tiger

Roar! Tigers are the biggest of all cats. They're known for their striped fur. Every tiger has a different pattern of stripes.

Orangutan

These red-haired apes spend most of their time in trees. They even sleep in nests above the ground.

Northern Tamandua

In rain forests, ants and termites go up into the trees. So do these small anteaters. They catch the insects with their sticky tongues.

Red-eyed Tree Frog

The tree frog has bright red eyes. Its eyes help scare away enemies that eat frogs.

Reticulated Python

This snake can grow up to 30 feet long—as long as some fire trucks! Pythons are good climbers and swimmers.

Toucan

The toucan is famous for its giant bill. Sometimes, a toucan's bill is as long as its whole body!

Boyd's Forest Dragon

This lizard catches insects on tree trunks. It sometimes has a favorite tree that it climbs again and again.

Jaguar

This spotted cat is mostly nocturnal, or awake at night. That's when the jaguar goes hunting.

Thoas Swallowtail Butterfly

What's one way to tell if it's a swallowtail butterfly? Look for the "tail," the long part on the back of the wings.

Macaws

These colorful birds live in big groups called flocks. In the rain forest, you can hear macaws squawking to each other—*caw caw.*